ISLAM

GLOBAL CITIZENS: WORLD RELIGIONS

Published in the United States of America by Cherry Lake Publishing
Ann Arbor, Michigan
www.cherrylakepublishing.com

Content Adviser: April C. Armstrong, Princeton University

Reading Adviser: Marla Conn MS, Ed., Literacy specialist, Read-Ability, Inc.

Photo Credits: © Antony McAulay/Shutterstock, cover, 1; © Sufi/Shutterstock, 5; © BEGY Production/Shutterstock, 6; © Jasminko Ibrakovic/Shutterstock, 8; © frees/Shutterstock, 11; © Marzolino/Shutterstock, 12; © Everett Historical/Shutterstock, 14; © Radiokafka/Shutterstock, 15; © Krunja/Shutterstock, 16; © Stefano Ember/Shutterstock, 19; © Everett – Art/Shutterstock, 20; © akturer/Shutterstock, 22; © Mansoreh/Shutterstock, 23; © Azraf Saip/Shutterstock, 24; © Tinxi/Shutterstock, 27; © dboystudio/Shutterstock, 28

Library of Congress Cataloging-in-Publication Data
Names: Marsico, Katie, 1980- author.
Title: Islam / by Katie Marsico.
Description: Ann Arbor, Michigan: Cherry Lake Publishing, 2017. | Series: Global citizens:
    world religions | Includes bibliographical references and index.
Identifiers: LCCN 2016033583| ISBN 9781634721561 (hardcover) | ISBN 9781634722223 (pdf) |
    ISBN 9781634722889 (pbk.) | ISBN 9781634723541 (ebook)
Subjects: LCSH: Islam—Juvenile literature. | Islam—History—Juvenile literature.
Classification: LCC BP161.3 .M3936 2017 | DDC 297—dc23
LC record available at https://lccn.loc.gov/2016033583

Cherry Lake Publishing would like to acknowledge the work of the Partnership for 21st Century Learning.
Please visit *www.p21.org* for more information.

Printed in the United States of America
Corporate Graphics

ABOUT THE AUTHOR

Katie Marsico is the author of more than 200 children's books. She lives in a suburb of Chicago, Illinois, with her husband and children.

TABLE OF CONTENTS

CHAPTER 1

History: Roots of the Religion

Since people began recording history, they have written about the idea of a power greater than themselves. Thousands of years later, various beliefs in this power continue to shape both individual lives and entire cultures. Religion is the system people use to organize such beliefs. Religion also standardizes ceremonies and rules for worship.

An Overview of Allah and His Prophets

Islam is the world's second-largest religion. Only **Christianity** has more followers. Members of the Islamic faith, or Muslims, believe in one **divine** being. They refer to him as *Allah*, which is Arabic for "God."

In Islam, there are several **prophets**. According to Muslims, Allah chose these men to help people understand and obey his

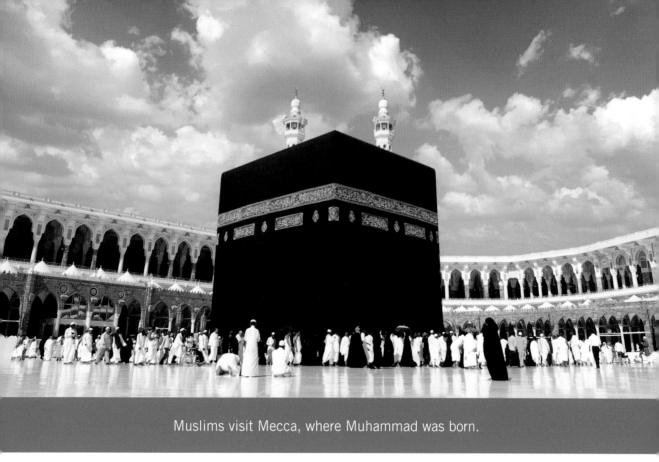

Muslims visit Mecca, where Muhammad was born.

laws. Some of the Islamic prophets are important figures in other religions, as well. Abraham and Moses are prophets in Islam, **Judaism**, and Christianity. To Muslims, Jesus of Nazareth has a similar role, but to Christians, Jesus is God as he came to earth, and his teachings form the basis of their faith. Muslims believe they have the best understanding of the same God that Jews, Christians, and Muslims all worship.

Muslims say a man named Muhammad was the final Islamic prophet. Historians think he was born in 570 CE in Mecca. In Muhammad's time, Mecca was a city in Arabia, which was a

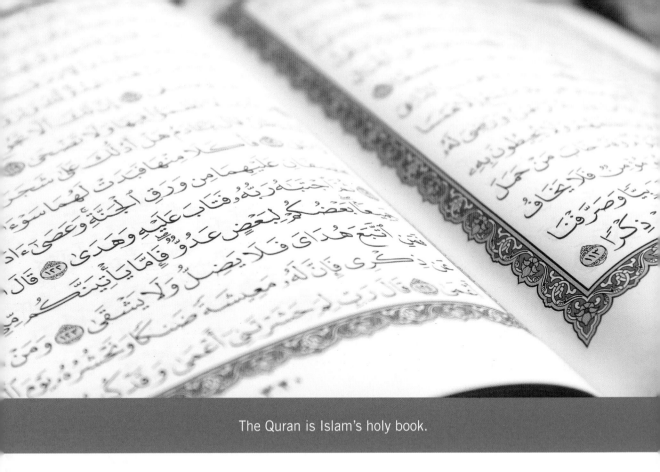

The Quran is Islam's holy book.

historic region in southwestern Asia. Arabia was made up of present-day Yemen and nations located along the Persian Gulf, including Saudi Arabia.

Unlike many of his fellow Arabians, Muhammad didn't worship more than one god. He had faith in a single divine being—the same one who had worked through Abraham, Moses, and Jesus. Muslims believe that Muhammad's **devotion** is why Allah chose to communicate revelations, or divine truths, to him. These revelations became the foundation of the Islamic faith.

Muhammad's Impact on Islam

Other prophets existed before Muhammad. Yet Muslims think that people altered, or changed, their messages over time. The revelations that Muhammad said he had received were seen as Allah's words in their purest form. Between 610 and 632—when Muhammad died—he shared what had been revealed to him. His ideas soon spread through much of Arabia.

By the end of the seventh century, Muslims recorded Allah's revelations to Muhammad in the Quran. The texts within the

Developing Questions

Why did early Muslims believe Muhammad when he said he had received revelations from Allah? What was Muhammad's life like before he became a prophet? What other religions were practiced in Arabia during the early seventh century?

The first question is a compelling question. Most compelling questions don't have straightforward answers, but many lead to interesting discussions and debates. The second and third questions are supporting questions. They have more clear-cut answers. People frequently use supporting questions to help form responses to compelling questions.

Devout Muslims pray five times a day.

Quran form the main collection of Islamic scriptures, or holy writings. Other important religious texts are found in the Sunna. The Sunna is an account of Muhammad's words and actions, as well as the stories of his companions.

Together, the Quran and the Sunna explain the beliefs and practices that make up the Islamic faith. They also describe the Five Pillars of Islam. These are ideas outlining what Muslims must do to lead **righteous** lives.

The first pillar is the *shahada*. The shahada involves Muslims reciting that there is only one God (Allah) and that Muhammad is his prophet. The second pillar is *salat*, or praying according to certain **rituals** five times a day. The third is *zakat*, or paying an **alms** tax that helps the poor. The fourth is *sawm*, or fasting from sunrise to sunset during Ramadan, the ninth month of the Islamic calendar. When Muslims fast, they do not eat or drink. The fifth pillar is the *hajj*, or a pilgrimage to Mecca. It is a holy journey that Muslims go on during Dhu'l-Hijja, the final month of the Islamic year.

A Look at Islamic Law

*Sharia, or Islamic law, is made up of religious codes that touch on every part of Muslims' lives. It is based on both scriptures and fatwas, which are judgments handed down by Islamic **scholars**. The rules within sharia address everything from trade to diet to marriage. This legal system features courts and a wide range of punishments for people found to be lawbreakers. In some cases, such individuals are even sentenced to death.*

CHAPTER 2

Geography: Mapping How Faith Formed

When Muhammad died in 632, his close adviser—Abu Bakr—became caliph. (The term *caliph* comes from the Arabic word *khalifa*, which means "successor.") Abu Bakr and the caliphs who followed him were considered both spiritual and political leaders. In the century after Muhammad's death, their armies seized control of a growing portion of the Middle East. Eventually, the Islamic Empire included Spain and parts of central Asia.

At first, most Muslims were Arab. As the Islamic Empire grew larger, however, other cultures started practicing Islam. Gradually, this religion spread among the Persians in western and southwestern Asia and the Berbers in North Africa.

Islam first spread around the Middle East.

For several centuries, the Ottoman Empire ruled the Middle East.

The Islamic Empire

In some areas, Muslims and members of other religions were able to live alongside each other with little conflict. Yet this wasn't always the case. Between the 11th and 13th centuries, Muslims and European Christians battled each other for ownership of Palestine. This historic region was located in the Middle East, along the eastern part of the Mediterranean Sea.

Ancient Palestine played an important role in the religious histories of both Islam and Christianity. Christians waged a series of crusades, or holy wars, in an effort to win control of the territory. Overall, they were unsuccessful.

From 1301 to 1922, Islam was the driving force behind the Ottoman Empire. Muslim Turks ruled this kingdom, which stretched across southwestern Asia, northeastern Africa, and southeastern Europe. Starting in 1453, Istanbul—which is located in modern-day Turkey—was the Ottomans' capital. It served as an important center of trade, politics, and Islamic worship.

Gathering and Evaluating Sources

History books aren't the only sources of information on the Islamic Empire. Art, architecture, maps, and literature also provide a closer look at how Islam developed across the globe. Members of the public are often able to view such items in museums and cultural centers. How do you think these sources are similar to reference books? How are they different? Why is it important to use a variety of sources when researching world religions?

Turkey entered World War One in 1914.

The Ottoman Empire crumbled not long after the end of World War I (1914–1918). Later, Europeans set up colonies in many former Islamic nations. Members of Islam struggled to preserve, or save, their way of life in certain areas. Some faced persecution, or poor treatment, from people who didn't share their religious beliefs.

A Rapidly Growing Religion

Throughout much of the 20th century, Muslims and members of other world religions continued to clash over common

Muslims and Hindus share different beliefs.

territory. For example, tension surrounded the division of India
into two different nations—Pakistan and India—in the 1940s.
Pakistan is home to mainly Muslims, while people living in India
are primarily **Hindus**. Disagreements over the borders separating
both countries still exist today. Similar conflicts erupt between
Palestinians, who are mostly Muslim, and their Israeli neighbors,
who are largely Jewish.

Nevertheless, Islam is currently the world's fastest-growing
religion. Researchers say 1.6 billion Muslims represent about 23
percent of the world's population. Of this number, roughly 62

Over half the people who live in Malaysia are Muslim.

percent live in Asian nations located on or near the western Pacific Ocean. Within the Asia-Pacific region, large populations of Muslims are found in Indonesia, India, Pakistan, Bangladesh, Iran, and Turkey.

Population Predictions

Between 2010 and 2050, the number of people who practice the Islamic faith is expected to grow by 73 percent! According to researchers, the world's Muslim population is likely to increase faster than the world's total population. They do not predict this will be the case for any other major religions within the same time period.

CHAPTER 3

Civics: Organization and Ideas

All Muslims share the same basic ideas about Allah, Muhammad, Islamic scriptures, and the Five Pillars of Islam. As Islam developed, however, it split into different subgroups, or sects. Many experts consider the two main Islamic sects to be Sunni and Shia.

Sunni

In most countries with large Muslim populations, Sunni is the more popular sect. (Exceptions are nations such as Iran, Iraq, and Lebanon.) Between 85 and 90 percent of Muslims are Sunni. When Muhammad died, Muslims who eventually formed this sect supported the idea of Abu Bakr becoming caliph. They thought that members of their faith community had the right to choose their leader.

These Sunni Muslims are praying in a mosque.

Sunnis frequently describe themselves as more traditional than Shiites. They believe their religious practices more closely reflect Muhammad's life and teachings. To Sunnis, Allah's power is obvious on Earth. From their point of view, he influences people's private, public, and political lives.

Shia

Unlike Sunnis, early Shiites did not consider Abu Bakr the leader. Instead, they argued that only a **descendant** of Muhammad was worthy of becoming caliph. They said that the

The caliph Ali died for his faith.

prophet had actually wanted his son-in-law and cousin, Ali, to succeed him.

Ali eventually did serve as caliph from 656 to 661. Later, he and his sons were **assassinated**. Even today, Shiites regard them as martyrs, or people who died for their faith. They refer to Ali—and all later caliphs who were related to him—as "imam." The imams inspired ideas about martyrdom and **sacrifice** that shape much of Shia. Some Shiites believe that dying for Allah is the ultimate sign of religious devotion.

Developing Claims and Using Evidence

In Islam, specific physical movements accompany salat. For example, Muslims raise their hands to their ears or shoulders to begin prayer. What are the purpose and meaning of these movements? (Hints: Do you think they help improve concentration? Do Muslims consider them good for their mind, body, spirit, or all three?) After developing an answer to the first question above, find facts to support your claim. Do your research at the library, online, or even at a local mosque. Just be cautious about reviewing information on the Internet. Some Web sites aren't reliable, although those operated by government agencies and colleges and universities usually are.

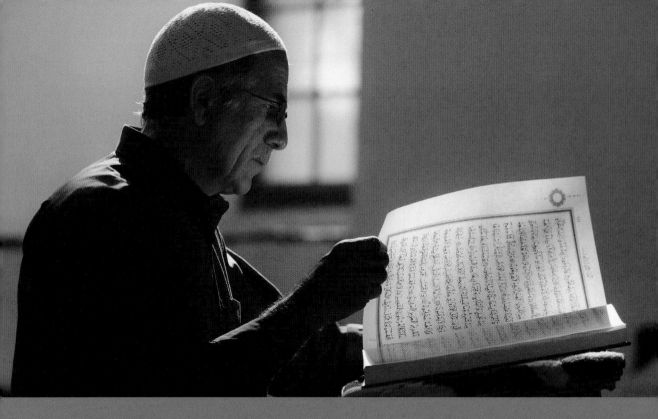

Imams are Muslim leaders.

Clergy and Ways of Worship

Islam features **clergy** known as ulama. Depending on their exact role, the ulama have different titles. For instance, muftis are scholars who help Muslims understand and observe Islamic family laws. In Shia, the highest-ranking ulama are called ayatollahs.

The ulama are sometimes also referred to as imams. To Sunnis, however, an imam is simply a clergyman. Sunni imams don't necessarily have to be related to Muhammad and Ali.

Muslims follow specific rules when they pray.

Muslim worship often occurs in buildings called mosques. Yet prayer is not restricted to this setting. What's more important is that Muslims pray five times a day. Beforehand, they clean themselves to ensure that their bodies and spirits are as pure as possible. Muslims always pray facing the shortest route to Mecca, which differs in direction depending on where they are in the world. Some people even have prayer mats with built-in compasses!

Muslims exchange gifts during Eid al-Fitr.

Celebrating Faith

In Islam, several holidays and festivals serve as opportunities for people to celebrate their beliefs. Some of the main Islamic holy days are described below.

Holiday	When It's Celebrated	Main Theme
Al-Hijra (Islamic New Year)	The first day of Muharram (the first month in the Islamic year)	Celebration of when Muhammad moved from Mecca to Medina and set up the first Islamic state
Ashura	The 10th day of Muharram	Day of remembrance when people recall martyrs who have died for the Islamic faith
Ramadan	Ramadan (the ninth month of the Islamic year)	Month of fasting that celebrates the period when Allah began revealing the wisdom of the Quran to Muhammad
Eid al-Fitr (Festival of the Breaking of the Fast)	The first three days of Shawwal (the 10th month of the Islamic year)	Celebration of the end of fasting (during Ramadan)
Eid al-Adha (Festival of the Sacrifice)	The 10th day of Dhu al-Hijja (the 12th month in the Islamic year)	Celebration of the prophet Abraham and his willingness to make sacrifices for his faith

Note: Based on the Islamic calendar, holidays and festivals sometimes occur during different seasons from year to year.

CHAPTER 4

Economics: Funding a Faith

Thanks to the ongoing faith of its members, Islam has existed for several centuries. Like all major religions, however, it relies on financial support, as well. Mosques require a certain amount of upkeep, or routine care. Additional funding is needed to run Islamic schools and **missions**.

Muslims believe in helping those in need. They perform a variety of charity work that aids the poor and hungry. Charitable efforts also include the operation of orphanages, clinics, and programming in areas affected by natural disaster.

Examples of Income

Zakat is one source of funding used to pay for charity projects and other expenses within Islam. It involves planned giving in

Muslims pay zakat to fund charity projects.

the form of a special tax. Muslims typically contribute 2.5 percent of their wealth every year. Some Muslims pay it in cash, and others pay with farming or mining products.

Most Muslims don't think of zakat as a charitable donation. According to Islamic scriptures, it is a requirement if they want to prove their obedience to Allah. Muslims also view zakat as a reminder that Allah decides if people are rich or poor.

Unlike zakat, sadaqah is money given voluntarily. Muslims see it as a way to please Allah, but they don't have to donate a set amount. Sadaqah is not among the Five Pillars of Islam.

Muslims live all over the world.

Taking Informed Action

Despite being the fastest-growing religion, Islam is often misunderstood and misjudged. Fortunately, education helps encourage religious tolerance, or acceptance. The first step is to continue learning about Islam and all major world religions. For starters, find out if you're able to visit nearby houses of worship. If possible, try to set up interviews with local religious leaders. Finally, talk to your family and friends about why it's important to respect people of all religions. If you practice an organized religion, this is also a good discussion to have within your own faith community. Take informed action to prove why the presence of different religious beliefs should be a source of celebration, not persecution!

An Amazing Past, Present, and Future

Zakat and sadaqah are just two examples of the traditions that shape Muslims' day-to-day lives. They are part of a faith rooted in a rich history and an incredible blend of people and places. As the world's fastest-growing religion, Islam is likely to remain a strong cultural influence in the world.

Communicating Conclusions

Think more about the concepts, or ideas, behind zakat and sadaqah. Then consider the sources of funding in other major religions. Do any require or request a regular payment from members? How do they encourage people to give freely?

A chart is a good way to organize the facts you find as you answer these questions. First, use a ruler to divide a sheet of paper or poster board into six columns. Label the columns with the names of the following world religions: Buddhism, Christianity, Hinduism, Islam, Judaism, and Sikhism. In each column, record information about taxes, dues (membership fees), or other methods of collecting funds.

Show your chart to family and friends. Discuss why money matters in religion. Also talk about how charity and the spirit of giving influence different faiths.

Think About It

According to researchers who conducted a worldwide survey, women who practice Islam have an average of three children. Meanwhile, non-Muslim women have an average of two. Also, on the whole, Muslims tend to be younger than members of other religious groups. Using this information and the knowledge that Islam is the world's fastest-growing religion, what are you able to conclude? How do you think family size and age affect a religion's population? Research statistics for other religions to find additional support for your claim.

For More Information

FURTHER READING

Ali-Karamali, Sumbul. *Growing Up Muslim: Understanding the Beliefs and Practices of Islam.* New York: Delacorte Press, 2012.

Blake, Philip. *My Religion and Me: We Are Muslims.* London: Hachette Children's Books, 2016.

Glossop, Jennifer, and John Mantha (illustrator). *The Kids Book of World Religions.* Toronto: Kids Can Press, Ltd., 2013.

WEB SITES

The Islamic Bulletin—Children's Corner
www.islamicbulletin.org/services/children.htm
Check out this Web site for videos, articles, and countless other online resources related to Islam.

IslamKids.org
www.islamkids.org/contents.html
Explore this Web site to learn more about Islamic beliefs and practices.

GLOSSARY

alms (AHLMZ) money, clothes, food, and other things given to poor people

assassinated (uh-SAS-uh-nated-id) murdered in a sudden attack often for political or religious reasons

Christianity (kris-chee-AN-ih-tee) the religion based on the life and teachings of Jesus

clergy (KLUR-jee) a group of people trained to lead religious groups, such as priests, ministers, and rabbis

descendant (dih-SEN-duhnt) someone who has a specific person or family among his or her ancestors

devotion (di-VOH-shuhn) strong feelings of loyalty and love

divine (dih-VINE) having to do with God

Hindus (HIN-dooz) followers of Hinduism, a religion and philosophy practiced mainly in India

Judaism (JOO-dee-iz-uhm) the religion of the Jewish people, based on a belief in one God and the teachings of the Torah

missions (MISH-uhnz) groups of people who travel to do an important job

prophets (PRAH-fits) people who speak or claim to speak for God

righteous (RYE-chuhs) without guilt or sin; morally good

rituals (RICH-oo-uhlz) acts that are always performed in the same way, usually as part of a religious or social ceremony

sacrifice (SAK-ruh-fise) the offering of something to God or a god

scholars (SKAH-lurz) people with a great deal of knowledge in a particular field

INDEX